Wiring Your Church for Worship

Abingdon Press & The Church of the Resurrection
Ministry Guides

Wiring Your Church for Worship

Constance E. Stella
Adam Hamilton, Series Editor

ABINGDON PRESS
Nashville

WIRING YOUR CHURCH FOR WORSHIP

This book is printed on acid-free paper.

Library of Congress Cataloging-in-Publication Data

Stella, Constance E.
Wiring your church for worship / Constance Stella.
p. cm.
ISBN 978-0-687-64281-6 (binding: pbk., adhesive perfect : alk. paper)
1. Church work–Audio-visual aids. 2. Public worship–Audio-visual aids. I. Title.

BV1535.S74 2007
264.0028'4–dc22

2007000401

07 08 09 10 11 12 13 14 15 16—10 9 8 7 6 5 4 3 2 1
MANUFACTURED IN THE UNITED STATES OF AMERICA

Contents

Foreword

In the early 1900s, churches did not have sound systems. Today few churches do ministry without them. Twenty years from now few churches will be without some form of media ministry. For churches interested in reaching tomorrow's young people, media will not be an option. Churches are in the business of proclamation and communication—we preach and teach the Good News. Media ministries allow us to do this in powerful new ways that have the potential to make our preaching and witness considerably more effective. The use of video interviews, classic art, film clips, maps and charts in preaching and worship have played a key role in helping to reach and disciple people at The Church of the Resurrection.

In *Wiring Your Church for Worship,* Constance Stella offers clear, helpful, and practical guidelines for starting or improving a media ministry in your church. As the person who started the media ministry at The Church of the Resurrection almost ten years ago, she knows what it takes to do this well. She understands the importance of deploying volunteers in this ministry.

I'm confident you will find this guide filled with helpful principles and practical ideas that will strengthen your media ministry.

••••••••••••••••••••••••••••••••••••

At The Church of the Resurrection, we live daily with the goal to help people become deeply committed Christians. More than nominally religious. More than the Sunday pew holder. More than the spectator. We know these same people become more by doing more. We begin with the knowledge that people want the church to be theirs. They want to know God has a place for them. With that in mind, we recognized from the very start that specialized ministries utilizing the skills and talents of laypeople are fundamental to church life.

A church on the move will have specialized ministries capitalizing on the skills and talents of laypeople. They are your keys to succeed.

In developing these guides, we listened to the requests of smaller churches for practical resources to enlist laypeople for this purpose. These economical guides, written by proven leaders at our church, will serve as essential resources for innovative, creative, and, more than likely, nontraditional church workers who have little or no budget to work with. With these guides in hand, your laypeople will be ready to plunge into the work with excitement and courage instead of tentatively approaching it on tiptoe.

At the core of these guides is the belief that anything is possible. It's a challenge, but it's a truth. God can and does use us all—with that conviction we bring hope to the world.

Adam Hamilton
Senior Pastor
The Church of the Resurrection
Leawood, Kansas

Chapter One

Starting Out or Starting Over

It's a new world. My video iPod proves it. And before that, the almost-hourly text messages from my teenagers on my cell phone proved it. And before that, the HDTV in my family room, which is so lifelike it's creepy, proved it. And before that, the wireless Internet connection that allows me to write this book from my screen porch proved it. And before that, the DVD player, which rendered boxes of VHS tapes useless. And before that, the twenty-four hour news channels, broadcasting news every minute, from every corner of the world. All the way back to the eight-track player in my high school boyfriend's Cutlass Supreme.

The world is "new" every few years, isn't it? The distance in time from the cool eight-track to the cool iPod is short—only a couple of decades. But what a difference in the way we give and take in information! What a difference in the way we communicate with each other, the way we tell what's important in our lives, the way we share our stories.

That's where you come in.

It sounds clichéd because we all say it all the time. But your task in the media ministry is to tell your church's story.

This guide is aimed at equipping you with the knowledge, tools, and strategies you need to get started. It begins with a look at your media ministry's foundation, then shows you how to build the ministry using both volunteers and paid staff, offers a few tips to help you create great media, and guides you through the basics of choosing equipment.

Two Foundational Principles

Whether you're just beginning to dream about using media in your church, or you're already leading a thriving media ministry, you must build on a firm foundation. Following are **two principles** that are critical to effective and sustainable media ministry. If you're just starting out, spend a couple of days thinking, praying, and working with others on a thorough consideration of these principles. If you're already well on your way in media ministry, set aside time each year to go back to these principles, to evaluate the strength of your foundation. (Note that the book, *Video Ministry: Using Media in Worship Without Going Hollywood* [Nashville: Abingdon Press, 2006] is a thorough explanation of these and other critical principles, including a series of questions about each, to guide you through an evaluation of your ministry.) You'll face many challenges, some of which might even threaten to knock the ministry off balance, to uproot it.

Use these principles to help keep your ministry Christ-centered, and it will grow to be like a tree *"planted along a riverbank, with roots that reach deep into the water. Such trees are not bothered by the heat or worried by long months of drought. Their leaves stay green, and then go right on producing delicious fruit"* (Jer. 17:8 NIV).

Principle 1: purpose

Your media ministry should have a clear purpose. That purpose should be above and beyond "making it easy for people to see the lyrics," or "bringing video into the service so more teenagers will come," or "everybody else is doing it, so we should too." The media ministry's purpose should extend directly out of the purpose of your church. It should be written out, in no more than a few sentences. It should be printed and posted where everyone might see it.

⇨ **Why** is purpose so important? Media ministry is still new in many churches. Congregants may not understand why they should support it. Unlike our colleagues in other ministry areas, there are very few networking organizations providing support and resources and models for media ministry. A clearly stated purpose helps everyone—including you—understand what the ministry is about and why it's important to your church. This is critical in

- building a ministry that makes good use of church resources,
- avoiding the unimportant projects syndrome,
- helping the church to grow,
- gaining and maintaining congregational support.

⇨ **How** can you define your purpose? Ideally, your church already has a written purpose statement, and everyone who's actively involved in the body knows it. If that's not the case, start with a conversation with your pastor or church council chairperson, or the people shaping the discussion of purpose in your church. Suggest a meeting or brainstorm session with church leaders to define and agree on a purpose statement. This is important for the whole church, not just the media ministry.

Get the church's purpose down on paper, and the media ministry's purpose will follow. If your church's purpose is "To share the gospel with unchurched people in our neighborhood," your ministry's purpose might be "To use video and other media as tools for sharing the gospel with unchurched people in our neighborhood." If your church's purpose is "To nurture Christian families through Bible study, Christian disciplines, and corporate worship," your ministry's purpose might be "To create media that aids in nurturing Christian families by providing media-based resources for Bible study and personal discipleship practices and by providing media and technical support for large group gatherings and weekend worship."

You will find a clear purpose helps you decide what to do—what projects are important, how to spend resources, where to concentrate efforts, what kind of equipment to invest in, and how to organize volunteers. It also helps define what *not* to do. In the media ministry area, the work is never done. It serves nearly every other area, either supporting technical needs for programming or producing media for worship and events. As a result, media ministries commonly spin out of control. A well-defined purpose helps keep your media ministry safely on track.

Principle 2: culture

If you're telling a story in French to a group of people who know only Chinese, is your storytelling effective? Of course not. The media ministry must speak your church's language and reflect a picture that's recognizable and authentic. Just as the media ministry's purpose should be a natural extension of the church's purpose, so should its work be integrally shaped by the church's culture. The church's culture is a snapshot of who the people are, what they're like, how they give and take in information; their commonalities, their shared needs, and their demographic profile.

Why is it important to consider your church's culture when building a media ministry? Simply put, because understanding that culture can make your storytelling effective. Your congregation is more comfortable with the media you produce, there's less resistance to it from the get-go. The congregation better understands the messages in your media and is compelled to action by them because the messages make sense to them. And people feel a positive sense of community because the media reflects who they are as a church in an authentic way. All of this helps the church to fulfill its purpose and to grow.

When we ignore our church's culture, we pour fuel on the fire for the folks who don't like media in church to begin with. If people say media doesn't belong in church, we've proven them right with media that doesn't seem to belong in *this* church. If the images are always edgy, hip-hop-styled in a church that's neither edgy nor hip (let alone *hip-hop!*), the congregants may be distracted and miss the point of worship entirely. If media reflects a picture of the church family that's too different from reality, the family may begin to feel uneasy, to be unsure about who they are, and may actually begin to fracture.

Getting a handle on the church's culture isn't difficult. Contact local government agencies and school districts to request demographic information for your area. Drive through the neighborhoods near your church and try to look at them with fresh eyes. Make notes of the trends you see. How do people live? What kinds of jobs do they have? What are their recreational habits? Contact the local paper and cable TV company and try to determine where your people like to get their information. Are they newspaper-readers, network TVwatchers, or podcast-downloaders? Pull together as much information as you can about the people your church serves.

- **Gather** a group of church or ministry leaders and together draw up a cultural profile of your congregation. From there, discuss what "language" your media should speak. What stylistic elements will work best? What styles might be a turn-off? What types of media will be most effective and expected? Simple lyrics and sermon points on still backgrounds or tons of video and web-based extensions? What sort of special effects will work with this audience? What sort of pacing will keep their interest without becoming distracting? Ask each other lots of questions and make good notes.

- **Create** a stylebook. This can be as detailed as you wish (and more detail is better than less). A stylebook is a document that sets the parameters for the look of your work. You'll determine what goes in your stylebook, and you'll probably add to it and alter it as time goes on. Here are a few ideas to get you started:
    1. Decide which fonts you will use and which ones should never see the light of day in your sanctuary.
    2. Decide what colors you will use and which ones (day-glow green, maybe?) you will avoid.
    3. Set clear guidelines for effects. ("Always use drop shadows, but only black ones," for example.)
    4. Determine the optimum length of videos for worship. I suggest you aim for one minute for most pieces and no more than three minutes for special projects. The exception might be stewardship and capital campaigns, where

you may need five minutes to tell a compelling story. **Five minutes should be the max for any video in worship.**

5. Set standards for font size in projected lyrics and for formatting of scripture passages, sermon points, and other text. Get down to the nitty-gritty: when to use italics or boldface type, what to center and what to justify left, where to put scripture references on screen, etc.

6. Publish your stylebook. Everyone who creates or uses media in your church should have a copy. And make sure the stylebook is kept updated.

- **Recognize** that you may be most comfortable in a *different* church culture than the one you're creating media for. But remember *Who* and *Why* you serve. Your aim should not be to express your own creative voice, although that may be the happy by-product sometimes. Your aim should be to express God's voice for your unique congregation. There's no more humbling or important calling, is there?

Taking Stock

You understand your ministry's **Purpose** and how to communicate in your church's **Culture**. You have set a strong foundation; now it's time to build (or rebuild) the media ministry. Once each year, spend time taking stock. Assess assets and resources. What skill-sets do staff and volunteers possess? What sort of equipment does the ministry have? How about the facilities? What other resources are there—positive attitudes, a collaborative church staff, an encouraging senior pastor? What is going well in the media ministry?

Next, scrutinize the ministry, looking for gaps, weak spots, missing pieces. If you're just starting out, you may see more liabilities than assets. That's okay; you'll soon see that balance begin to shift.

Hold a daylong long-term planning session.

- **Invite** four to eight others. The list should include people who are stakeholders or collaborators in the media ministry—volunteers, staff, your pastor, the music director.
- **Invite** one additional person to serve as facilitator; this should be someone who is objective and has no agenda; ideally, it is someone who has led meetings like this before, who can keep the group sharing openly without getting bogged down. You should not facilitate your own planning session.
- **Set up** a meeting place that will be comfortable for this long meeting. Make sure there's food and drink, including lunch, for the participants. Use giant flip-chart paper to record all the responses and designate one person as scribe.

Devote the first part of the session to the stock-taking questions discussed above. Other issues that need to be addressed should be big issues, requiring problem-solving strategy, such as establishing a process between music and the tech team for graphics production. Don't waste planning session time on small things that just need to get done, such as equipment repairs.

After you have listed all the major assets, liabilities, and issues, it's time to boil that information down to the essence. Keeping **Purpose** and **Culture** in mind, the group should review the information on the flip charts. What are the most important points? What points appear over and over? What points are least significant? What rises to the top?

Together, agree on distinct objectives to address the most critical issues. Don't take on more than five or six objectives at a time. Assign a due date and one owner to each objective; it's the owner's responsibility to make sure the objective is met. He or she should determine how to get the job done, but that doesn't mean the owner does all the work. The objectives should leverage your assets and minimize the effect of your liabilities. They should help you stay purpose-centered, speaking effectively in your church's culture and working with excellence.

Media ministry leaders often complain that their ministries seem out of control. It's tough to carve out time for this sort of long-range planning, but it's one of the best ways to bring—and keep—the media ministry under control.

Your Pastor's Voice

I get this question often: "What's it *really* like to work with Adam Hamilton?" Media ministry folks generally ask because they are wondering how to navigate the working relationship with the pastor. This is apparently tricky territory; the questions come up at every Leadership Institute and every time I meet with media ministry colleagues. Every pastor and every media producer is different. They work differently, think differently, and communicate differently. While there isn't a simple list of rules to ensure a productive and healthy relationship with your pastor, here is a representative list.

Some rules to help relationships.

- **Understand** the pastor's intention and trust one another. Know your pastor's heart. Know him or her as a person. Build trust between you. When you face a stressful time, you will both need to rely on that trust. It is irreplaceable.

- **Learn** the pastor's voice. Media ministry people are the pastor's chief communicators. You're the megaphone, the canvas, the storyteller. Your voice must match the pastor's voice. You must learn the words, rhythms, phrases, pacing, and style of the pastor. You must hear the music that resonates most completely with your pastor. You must observe which colors, images, fonts, and other visual elements the pastor appreciates most. There may be times when you would rather "speak" in your own voice, and there may be a time when that is appropriate. But when you represent the pastor with your work, when you are speaking for him or her, you must do that in a way that's authentic to the pastor.
- **Own** the pastor's God-given vision. Your pastor is the chief vision caster of your church. That is a critical role. You play an important part in that. So you must understand that vision and carry it in your heart. You should be able to articulate it as clearly as the pastor does—in fact, that's probably part of your job. Your pastor should be passionate and sold out to God's call for your church, and so should you.

- **Make** the pastor your priority. This is a pretty simple concept. In the service of God, the pastor and worship should be the first priority for the media team.
- **Bolster** the pastor's strengths. What is your pastor good at? How can you use media to emphasize that, to leverage it for great teaching and preaching? That may mean creating humorous videos for a pastor who's a funny guy, or using dramatic lighting for an intense storyteller, or lots of graphics for a visually organized teacher. Only you know what works best for you and your pastor. If your pastor is hesitant to use media, you will need to lead. Show examples from other churches. Set up

a time for the pastor to "practice" using graphics or video, to get a feel for it, so he or she can begin getting comfortable. Rehearse anything new or unusual before worship, so the pastor feels good about how the element works. Be careful to ease the pastor into media slowly, if necessary. Fight your own sense of impatience, if necessary, to empower you pastor. The flip side of this concept is to urge your pastor away from anything that is likely to trip him or her up or something the pastor probably will not be able to pull off effectively. If your relationship is built on trust, your pastor will come to rely on you to keep from becoming the emperor with no clothes!

- **Show** the pastor what the media ministry needs. Most pastors have no training in media production, no idea what's required to produce a video or a graphics sequence. So before you utter the next complaint about the pastor's unrealistic demands, ask yourself this question: have I explained to the pastor in a way that can be understood exactly what is required to do this work? Some pastors are pretty hands-off and don't really get close enough to a project to understand what's involved. In this case, schedule some time for the pastor to shadow you through several parts of the process. Write out the average time it takes to do each task. This should not be used as a tool for confrontation. Your pastor will almost certainly want to understand what is being asked—assume that's the case.
- **Honor** the pastor's boundaries. Know what the pastor needs to do his or her job and honor that. Don't be a space invader. Don't corner the pastor on Sunday morning to rattle off a list of things to think about. Don't get the pastor involved in technical

issues unless it's absolutely necessary—especially not just before worship services begin. Know the pastor's work style and any unique limitations and do your best to work within them, giving up futile attempts to change the pastor's style to meet yours. Don't push the pastor to use technical tools or media that he or she is not comfortable with.

- **Move** ahead on the pastor's plans. If your pastor is planning sermons by series—and is planning them several months out—you're among the lucky few! One of the best things for the media ministry to do is to move forward on the things that are certain. If there will be a graphic sequence during the Anthem next month, get working on it now. Work ahead on anything that you are 85 percent certain will happen as planned. Then . . .
- **Remain** flexible to respond to the pastor's heart. If you've nailed down everything you can, you should have the flexibility to respond to last-minute changes and inspirations with less stress.
- **Support** the pastor. This one is simple too. In everything you say and do, you should support your pastor. If there is anything that concerns you or if you have a question that makes you unsure how to respond to others on behalf of the pastor, go to the pastor and talk about it. And if conversations with the pastor are unsatisfactory or unproductive? One of the strengths of connectional churches like The United Methodist Church is the structures and processes to rely on when things (or people) go wrong. If you have concerns about your pastor's skills, capabilities, or conduct, pursue resolution the right way—honorably, within the channels set up in the church system.

Chapter Two

Organizational Models

It's easier if I just do it myself.
I'm the only one the pastor trusts.
I don't have time to teach someone else the skills.
This job is too important; I'm the only one who can do it right.
There's no one else in the church who's willing to do this stuff.

Fess up. You've said or thought one of the above at some point in your ministry, right? We all have; I've been guilty of every one on the list. But at some point, you must realize two key realities about media ministry:

1. A church could never afford to pay for enough media staff. A church could try, but the media ministry would never grow, and your church would suffer. It would be a brilliant example of horrible stewardship.

2. You are privileged to be responsible for a piece of God's ministry on this earth. As such, God requires you to care for and serve with God's people. And God is faithful, providing what we need to do this work. If you attempt to do

ministry alone, or with people whose primary aim is a paycheck, you rob others of the opportunity to serve, you deny yourself the blessing of serving with selfless others, and you withhold full faith in God, honoring God halfheartedly.

The use of volunteers in media ministry is the only sustainable way, and it is the best—most fun, most rewarding, most dynamic, most potential-filled—way to operate a church media ministry.

Work in Teams

One of the most important steps the person heading up the media ministry can take is to organize teams. This should be done no matter how many people are serving in the ministry, no matter what sort of work everyone does. The simple fact is that to sustain and grow the media ministry, people must work in teams.

At Resurrection, our media ministry wasn't formed into teams until several years after our inception. When you're just starting out, running a "seat-of-your-pants" ministry, it's easy to think you don't need to put energy into forming teams, that it's smarter to just get the work done, all hands on deck. Don't make that mistake. We burned people out and were less effective because we didn't put the effort into team formation.

Organization

Teams can be organized in a couple of different ways: by task or by time of service. Each structure has advantages. At Resurrection, we organized teams by task for a time, then switched to a time-of-service team structure. Volunteers and folks in other departments of your church can make suggestions. Find out what's worked and what hasn't. Your church might already have guidelines in place for structuring volunteer teams; if so, take advantage of any resources available.

- **Task-based** teams seem to work well for ministries that are just starting out or that have relatively few volunteers. This organizational structure helps to develop momentum. If potential volunteers see that there's some organizational strength and mass behind the graphics team, for instance, they will be more likely to sign on. They see that there are others who will help them learn, others who might become their friends, others who have chosen to serve in this way. Pretty soon, you might go from a graphics team of three people to a graphics team of six! This type of structure also helps younger ministries develop volunteer skills. You can concentrate on training new sound techs, for instance, if you form a team just for those volunteers. We all learn and grow in groups. In a task-based team, volunteers share ideas, demonstrate techniques, and motivate one another to do better. Try forming one team at a time, starting with the area where volunteers' skills need to be developed.
- **Time-based** teams typically work well for media ministries that support multiple worship services and events each week and that have many volunteers. Scrambling to fill crew rosters for worship services and other events is an indication that you might need to form time-based teams. Volunteers should commit to serving the same time each week (or biweekly). They should find their own subs when they're unable to serve.

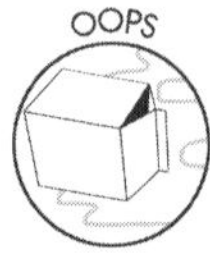

At Resurrection, the full-time staff hesitated to ask volunteers to commit to a time and to commit to the responsibility of finding their own subs. We delayed this move for a couple of years and found we were spending valuable staff and volunteer hours on the phone and e-mail each week filling in gaps. After the change, a mini-transformation occurred in the ministry. Volunteers had a new sense of ownership in the ministry and were faithful to their new responsibilities.

Another advantage of time-based teams is the consistency you can develop in production. Volunteers begin to really work together well when they're with the same people week after week. They anticipate each other's moves and can cover for each other's mistakes. Over time, the worship media will be smoother and better because of well-jelled, time-based teams.

When planning for big events like Christmas and Easter services, you will need extra teams, right? Several months ahead of time, each team should select one event to do as a team. So, for instance, the 10:30 a.m. Sunday crew might choose to do the 11:00 p.m. Candlelight Christmas Eve service together. Teams like this process and it works!

Team leaders

When forming teams, there's one critical component: leaders. The person heading up the media ministry (whatever the title) should make sure to appoint one leader for each team. Leaders make the team system work. They are primarily responsible for communication. Without a good leader, the teams will eventually fall apart or become dysfunctional. It's important that you invest the time and energy required to find and place effective leaders on each team.

- **Appoint** only one leader per team. At Resurrection, we've tried coleadership models, and they never seem to work. Leaders must be able to accept the role fully. Cracks develop in coleader models, and you know what happens when there are cracks in the system: things fall through!

- **Don't assume** that the best leaders are those who are most skilled technically. The guy who's a whiz on the audio board may actually be the worst candidate for sound team leader. Instead, make the technical whiz the volunteer trainer. Or ask him or her to write a tip sheet for volunteers or take responsibility for repairs and maintenance of the gear. Occasionally, the whiz really is the best leader; that's a bonus.
- **Look** for simple leadership qualities. Leaders should first be growing, committed Christians. They should be good listeners. They should understand and be fully committed to the mission of the church and ministry, with no hidden agenda. They should be emotionally healthy people, with good relationships. They should be organized, with good skills in follow-through and administration. They should be effective communicators. They should be comfortable with change. They should be positive and able to influence others in positive ways. They should be people-lovers, good at working with just about any type of person. They should be unabashedly supportive of the church's leadership as a whole.

- **Give** leaders real responsibility. Set guidelines and parameters, but allow leaders to make important decisions. They should know clearly which decisions are theirs to make. Encourage leaders to delegate some tasks so they are free to invest meaningfully in their teams. Leaders should feel (and truly be) fully vested in the ministry, responsible for its successes and failures.
- **Take** care of leaders. Nurture and develop them, in particular. Hold an annual anointing ceremony to recast the ministry's vision for its leaders, offering a time for them to prayerfully recommit to their roles. The person who heads up the media ministry should send thank-you notes to leaders or take them to lunch or out for coffee. Team leaders will become great blessings.

Communication

It is impossible to overcommunicate to media ministry volunteers. The person heading up the media ministry is responsible for this. Use a communication system that works for the majority of the people in the ministry, and require volunteers and staff to use it. At Resurrection, out of 200 people, at last count only one did not have a reliable e-mail account. Every volunteer provides an e-mail address upon sign-up for the ministry.

E-mail reigns supreme at Resurrection.

- **Use** the system consistently; rely on other means of communication, too, but mainly for special events or notices. For instance, send invitations for the annual leadership retreat via snail mail.

- **Provide** every volunteer with a full roster. It should include name, volunteer position, team, and all contact information. A volunteer or staff person should be responsible for keeping this document up-to-date and for sending a current version periodically.
- **Team leaders** are critical to the communication system's success. Members on every team should know their leader and should know how to contact him or her. The reverse is also true; leaders should know their team members, and how to contact them.

- **Team leaders** should be tasked with passing on all communication from the ministry staff. The reverse is true here too. Leaders should gather information (personal joys and concerns, ministry ideas, issues needing to be addressed) from their team members, and should pass that back to the staff.
- **One person,** probably a staff member if there is paid staff, should be designated as the point person for team leaders. That person should keep every leader fully informed, and should be the go-to-person on staff for the leaders.
- **Diagram** the communication system in some way so that everyone can see exactly how it works and what's expected.
- **Help** volunteers understand *why*. The head of the media ministry should be able to explain the context of decisions made, of church policies, of the ministry's expectations. Background will help volunteers to be vested in reaching the ministry's goals.
- **Don't assume** volunteers will remember all details. Provide tools to help them.

Tools for Volunteers

- **Send** the worship order with all technical cues on Friday before each weekend's services.

- **Make** laminated start-up checklists, showing each detailed task required to start up your media system. Make a checklist for shutdown too. And make a checklist for each position on your team—camera, graphics operator, video operator, etc. Keep these tools *at the workstation* and DON'T let them be removed.
- **Make** a laminated troubleshooting checklist for each major piece of equipment and for each volunteer workstation. Take digital photos of the equipment, showing what it means for the "Power" toggle to be set to "On." I needed to fill in at the lighting board for a sick volunteer one Sunday, and I could not figure out how to turn the system on. I had to call the poor sick volunteer at home to get instructions!

- **Create** a newsletter, aimed at the folks in the media ministry. Invite a volunteer from the church—someone who enjoys writing and desktop publishing—to serve as editor/publisher. Print volunteer profiles, with interesting tidbits about them. Print favorite recipes from the latest ministry potluck. Print a brief devotional, related to media ministry. Print schedules, calendars, staff and volunteer leader contact information, and whatever else makes sense for the teams. At Resurrection, the newsletter is distributed via e-mail to all volunteers; printed copies reside in the media ministry office, the media room, and the meeting room.

- **Remember** that the single most powerful method of communication is face-to-face. Hold quarterly team leader meetings, where leaders can encourage each other and share ideas. This is also a great format for long-term planning and problem solving. Hold an all-ministry meeting at least once each year; more often if possible. Share all the ministry news, the church's vision for where God is leading the ministry, remind volunteers of their commitment and of the ministry's expectations, and enjoy fellowship. Most importantly, hold team meetings every time the team comes together to serve, if they're time-based teams. Hold meetings monthly if the teams are task-based.

➪ **Caution**: e-mail is convenient but dangerous. Don't use it to communicate anything that's laced with emotion—especially anger or frustration. Don't use it to disseminate long or complicated policy or news of a big change. The head of the media ministry should print this information and call the volunteers together to review it in person, where they will be able to ask questions and get familiar with the issue. E-mail is good for brief, straightforward, factual information. Pick up the phone or schedule a meeting for the rest.

Spiritual Nurturing

There's one question that's more important than anything for your media ministry. My friend and colleague, Frank Gentile, first asked it in 2002, and I'll never forget it: "Is God in your gizmo?" In the media ministry, you should not forget this either. It may be the most important way you serve Christ in your ministry.

Consider this: many of the people who volunteer to serve in media ministry would not volunteer anywhere else. They would not teach children's Sunday school, or sing in the choir, or lead a Bible study class. They volunteer in media ministry, at least in part, because it seems "safe" from religious intimidation. They figure they won't be asked to share their testimony before others, quote a favorite scripture, or explain a theological concept.

What does this tell you about these volunteers? It should tell you that some of them are new-to-the-faith, infant Christians. And how do you interact with an infant? You take care of it, nurture it, help it to grow.

Notes for the media ministry leader

- **Model** the life of a deeply-committed Christian. Do the things you know you're to do as a follower of the Lord. If your church has any sort of covenant or guidelines for spiritual growth and behavior, follow them closely. If your church doesn't provide this tool, create your own. Write a set of expectations, covering things like drug and alcohol abuse; participation in small groups or Bible study; healthy relationship with colleagues, volunteers, and family; personal devotion and the practice of spiritual disciplines. What are the Christian codes of conduct you desire to live by? Write them down and humbly live by them. And share them with volunteers.
- **Take** full advantage of your church's programs for spiritual development. Encourage volunteers to sign up for these programs. Host a special *Disciple* Bible study sign-up party just for media ministry folks. Nominate promising volunteers for the church's leadership development programs. They will feel honored and will grow spiritually in leadership.
- **Foster** healthy relationships among the volunteers. As they work in teams, set up simple processes for them to relate to one another. Share joys and concerns in the preservice meeting, for instance.
- **Provide** regular opportunities for volunteers to experience Christian community. Hold volunteer-organized movie nights, hayrides, cookouts, and other fun activities. If many volunteers have kids, be sure to plan a couple of kid-friendly parties.

➪ **Lead** volunteers on a spiritual retreat once each year. Plan the retreat months in advance, so folks can get it on their calendars. Spend a night away at a regional church camp. Plan a devotional for evening and morning. Spend some time doing long-range planning or other "big idea" work involving volunteers. Prepare and eat a meal together. Invite guests to present a topical seminar. Invite a pastor to share Holy Communion or to anoint the teams.

A note on church camps: these are located all across the country; most United Methodist Church conferences have a camp and will rent it to church groups for small fees. Some even provide meals and extras like bonfires, hayrides, and seminars. For many of the volunteers attending, this will be the very first time they've experienced anything like this. For me, the annual retreat is one of my most treasured ministry activities.

CHAPTER THREE

Volunteer 101

There's only one way to get church members to join as volunteers in media ministry: ask! The personal invitation of one friend to another is the single most important source of volunteers at Resurrection. Create a ministry where people can serve in a way that's meaningful, nurturing, challenging, and fun, and they will bring their friends and neighbors and spouses and children to serve too.

There's a classic Kansas City hamburger joint just north of Resurrection's church building. During the writing of this book, a group of production staff and volunteers gathered there to talk about the project's content. I invited these friends and colleagues to share their wisdom about media ministry. The combined total experience in the group is well over one hundred years! After we had ordered, we settled in to talk. I asked the group, "What's the single most important thing I should share with the readers of this ministry guide?" At once, almost in unison, everyone answered, "Volunteers!"

So, for a multitude of good reasons, the media ministry is a place for volunteers. They are indeed important. Whether you're a volunteer yourself or paid staff heading up volunteers, the following discussion should be a good springboard for ideas.

Recruiting Reminders

- **Make** sure your "house" is in order. Be organized. Have a way to record the contact information of any person who expresses even slight interest in the media ministry. Return phone calls. Keep your roster up to date. Know your organization backward and forward.

- **Have** a clear process for taking people into the ministry. Who is their first contact? How do they get trained? How much time do they have to learn the job? What's their first task? Who will be their team leader? What happens if they can't do the job or decide they don't want to? What's required of them as media ministry volunteers? Who should they talk to if they have a problem or concern? *Explain all these things to each new recruit, in person. And know the answers to their questions!*
- **Ask** them to complete a new volunteer information sheet the moment they express a desire to volunteer. This should include bio and contact information, plus birthdays, family member names, special skills and interests, and any pertinent experience.
- **Put** the team structure, expectations of volunteers, volunteer and staff covenants, contact information, and any other important information on paper. Put it into the hands of every person who might be interested in the media ministry.

- **Use** technology itself as a recruiting tool. Set up a camera and monitor on the church lawn. You will attract every kid for miles around—and their parents. Have attractive recruiting pieces ready to give to potential volunteers. Staff the station with happy and energetic volunteers who like to talk about the ministry. Have a long sheet of blank paper ready for sign-ups!

- **Recruit** families and couples actively. If one spouse is not interested or capable to serve in a technical position, recruit him or her for a nontechnical post. At Resurrection, we have had volunteers who bake for crew call meetings, write and send birthday cards to volunteers, serve as gophers for big events, do database entry compiling orders for sermons on CD/DVD and mail those orders, plan all-ministry parties, and participate in many other nontechnical tasks. Teenagers and their parents make great team members together. The kids usually are more skilled and learn faster than their moms and dads. So parents learn humility, and teens learn patience. It's a win-win!

- **Recruit** at local colleges, ad agencies, and TV stations. These are great sources for students and young professionals who are looking for ways to build a portfolio of work. Offer projects for pay, if you can. Offer internships (typically unpaid in media professions) in the summer—these give interns a chance to do real work for their resume and portfolio. Sometimes there are camera operators and editors working at TV stations who want to work on something as a change of pace from house fires and robberies. And they might do this work for your church at drastically reduced costs. Pick up the phone and make some calls, especially if you have a specific project (a capital campaign, maybe?) that you need professional help with.
- **Offer** fun enticements. At Resurrection, we keep barrels of Twizzlers and M&Ms in the media workspaces. These have become the official "food" of our ministry. And from the very beginning, we offered T-shirts, ball caps, sweatshirts, and coffee mugs to volunteers, all emblazoned with the Saving Grace Productions (The Church of the

Resurrection media ministry) logo. These touches add a sense of fun, camaraderie, and healthy pride for volunteers.

On Recruiting Youth

For some teens, the media ministry is one place where they are truly comfortable in church. They've grown up with technology; it's second nature for them, so they're ideal recruits. Many teens also have free time, so they're able to take up some slack in your ministry. To keep in mind:

1. I recommend that you *not* recruit anyone under the age of 14. And be very clear that you will *consider* teenage recruits. They may apply for a volunteer position but are not assured of getting on the team until they are 18.
2. Do a careful personal interview with the child before you agree to sign him or her on.
3. Discuss the ministry's expectations with both the child and a parent—in person.
4. If accepting a teenage volunteer, immediately pair him or her with an adult partner. This person should be on the teen's team and should serve as trainer and mentor. Ideally, the team leader takes this role.
5. Important: before you accept teenage volunteers, check with the church staff about any child protection policies. Make sure you understand them and comply with them completely. These policies may prevent you from allowing volunteers under the age of 18.

Volunteer Development

Once they're in the front door, how do volunteers get trained? Training and skill development are the nuts and bolts of the media ministry.

Some volunteer ideas to consider:

- **Volunteers** in technical positions during worship should serve at least twice per month. Otherwise they get rusty, and mistakes proliferate.
- **Volunteers** should be on a regular rotation, for instance, serving every other Sunday at 9:00 a.m. If you have more than one worship service each weekend, consider asking volunteers to serve at each service on "their" weekend. This works especially well with two services. The volunteers' skills improve quickly with this extra practice, and your production will get smoother and better. If there are more than two services, it might be difficult to get volunteers to commit to the entire weekend. One thing you might try if you have three or more services: ask volunteers to commit to the entire weekend, but only every third week. At Resurrection, we've found three weeks to be a sort of sweet spot, where volunteers' skills remain strong, but their time commitment is manageable.

IDEA TO TRY

- **Plug** people in at the simplest and most risk-tolerant position first. If you run multiple cameras for I-Mag, put new people there. If they struggle, there is always another camera to go to. If a person claims to have skill in a particular area (computers, say) give him or her an opportunity to demonstrate that skill in a noncritical setting before assigning a specific post. Observe a training session or music tech rehearsal, for instance, to see if the guy who says he's a computer whiz really *is*.
- **Always** do initial training one-on-one, person-to-person.
- **Training** for most positions should be three, one-on-one sessions, one or two observation sessions (where trainees sit in the booth, headset on, watching and

listening), and finally on-the-job sessions with a trainer or full volunteer standing by for bail-out. Communicate your training process before it starts, so the trainee knows what to expect. The training process should be individualized. Some people will need more time than I've described here. Others will need much less.

- **Trainers** should have top-notch technical skills, an abundant supply of patience, and excellent abilities to work with all sorts of people. Whenever possible, use volunteers as trainers. They naturally empathize with the trainee, which makes the trainee feel welcomed and part of the team immediately. Trainers should communicate each recruit's progress to the appropriate staff and team leaders, so everyone knows when to expect the newest member.

- **Celebrate**. Do something to mark a new recruit's entry into the ministry. Throw a mini-party at the newbie's first crew meeting. Ask all the team members to share something about themselves. Every six months, do a quiet anointing ceremony for the volunteers who have joined the ministry that term. Or stage a lighthearted "graduation ceremony," complete with printed diplomas and canned "Pomp and Circumstance."

Skill development paths

Most people want to grow and improve. It's the leader's task to help make that happen. **Write out** a list of each specific skill you would like the best volunteers to have for each position. For example, the camera operator list will include everything from "Hold a steady shot" to "Zoom from wide shot to close-up, while adjusting framing and keeping tight focus, smoothly and slowly." Next, **break the list** into three Skill Levels. Skill Level 1 should include the basic skills you would expect a volunteer to possess after being on the job for a couple of months. Skill Level 2 should include the next level of skills, describing a volunteer who's proficient and reliable, the bread and butter volunteer you want on each team. Skill Level 3 should include the top tier of skills, describing the best volunteers imaginable, those with professional-grade talents.

As you can imagine, this can be a tedious task. To get it done, gather team leaders or others and work through the lists for each job as a group. You'll compile more complete lists and finish faster.

Publish the Skill Development Levels. Require your trainers to discuss them with trainees (but not at their first session—you will scare them off). Don't put someone in a regular position until they're able to demonstrate proficiency in Level 1 skills.

- **Team** leaders should encourage volunteers to work on their skills to increase proficiency.
- **Trainers** should be available to work with those volunteers who want to "move up."
- **Group** training sessions should be held at least once each year. A good time to do this is during music rehearsals when mistakes are okay, but there are graphics to run and something to shoot (if you use cameras). Use these sessions as opportunities to increase volunteers' skill levels.
- **Use** Skill Levels to motivate volunteers and to provide consistent quality in your event production. When planning events or worship, determine what skill level is required for each position. If it's a major worship event, with lots of challenges (the Christmas Extravaganza, perhaps?), you might designate several positions as Level 2 or even Level 3. When you put together the crew for that event, you know what you're looking for and can communicate that to the volunteers. The ones who want to learn and grow will aspire to those big events and will work to get there.

The pink slip

Once upon a time, we had a volunteer who was uninterested in improving his skills beyond barely basic. As he settled into his volunteer job, he developed a sort of arrogant complacency. He seemed to figure the church was lucky he showed up every few weeks. Another volunteer gently but firmly coached him one Sunday after another lackadaisical performance. He resented the unrequested help and retorted, "What are they going to do? *Fire* me?"

Yes, actually. Now and then the head of the media ministry will find a volunteer who, for one reason or another, is not performing up to the necessary level. The best approach is *not* to "fire" volunteers, of course, but to help them move from failure to success. Know that sometimes, however, the choice may indeed be to give the proverbial pink slip.

Following are some "case studies" and suggested solutions:

Territorialism

Jack's been running sound ever since God invented microphones, or so it seems. Sure, he's an amateur, but he practically built the church's system himself. Nobody else knows where everything is or understands his patching process. He accepts help from a high school kid sometimes, but the kid is really only good for dusting off the board, pulling up cables, that sort of thing, or so Jack thinks. Jack can't trust other people to do anything important; there's too much risk that they would just mess up his system.

His system. It's easy for us to develop "Jacks" in our ministries. Those great volunteers who want to dive in and take ownership, who will devote extraordinary time and energy, who look for ways to make things better. We treasure our "Jacks." But sometimes their sense of ownership deepens into territorialism. "Protecting" becomes all-important. When change needs to occur in the ministry, it can be difficult to work with someone so entrenched. A few ideas to try: invite participation. Explain the vision for where you think the ministry needs to be, and why it's important. Then ask Jack to brainstorm with you, to generate ideas for how you might get there. If you can help Jack see the need for change, he might lift himself right out of self-protection mode in order to be part of the action.

Lack of Understanding

Susie serves faithfully in her position as graphics formatter. She's enthusiastic and positive. She hardly complains when the lyrics are chosen late some weeks, and she always gets the graphics sequence put together on time, no matter what gets thrown in at the last minute. Problem is, Susie loves clip art and the color pink. The stylebook that has been created is based on the church's culture, aimed at helping fulfill your church's purpose. The stylebook is part of the definition of excellence for the ministry. And there are no clip art figures nor any shades of pink in your stylebook. You've mentioned the stylebook to Susie and the other volunteers, and it's sitting on the shelf near the graphics workstation. But nearly every Sunday, there they are: cutesy little line drawings, and lyrics floating in a fuschia sea.

Susie wants to serve your church well, but she needs help in understanding what that means. Reiterate important points in some way at least once each quarter; work them into your presentation at meetings, lift them up in prayer before services, include a monthly "Vision" column in the ministry newsletter. Be directive and decisive with volunteers, especially those like Susie. Don't just mention expectations and hope volunteers will take the hint. Set up a time to specifically walk them through. Explain the parameters and why they're important. Show them examples of what's okay and what's not. It's the leader's task to bring them along, to make sure they understand and envision those standards themselves.

Lack of Skill

Thomas was a prize recruit. When you met him, you were bowled over by his passion for the ministry and his desire to be part of wherever God leads it. You were just beginning to use two video cameras, recording the sermons for DVD, and Thomas was thrilled when you offered him a spot as camera operator. He struggled a bit through training, but you were sure he would settle in. After months of patient coaching and hours of retraining, however, Thomas is not progressing. His framing is still off-kilter, his pans are jerky, and every zoom-in makes you woozy. Nothing seems to improve his skills. He realizes this is a problem and apologizes profusely. Yet he doesn't give up and remains committed to the ministry.

Volunteers like Thomas are a huge blessing, but present leaders with a quandary. We don't want to lose these people who are our friends, who are encouraging to us and to others, who have the right heart for ministry. At the same time, we have a job to do, and we can't let a bad situation linger. If mistakes are consistently distracting the congregation in worship, we must make a change. And why would we keep putting valued people in a place where we know they will fail and where they'll have to deal with all the fallout from that failure over and over again?

Your first and best step in this situation is to look for an alternative place for that person to serve. It may be an open position of another kind, or an area where you need additional team members. Or it may be a position that you haven't even thought of yet! Thomas might be a lousy camera operator, but there's certainly a need in the ministry that he can fill, a place where he will succeed and propel your ministry in a new way. This story has played out many times in the life of the media ministry at The Church of the Resurrection.

Consider the volunteers individually. What do you know about them that might provide clues to their giftedness? What *are* they good at? What in their personality points to a strength you might capitalize upon? In the case of Thomas, maybe he struggles on camera because he is not physically calm; maybe he needs to be doing things that require a strong and forceful hand rather than a steady and gentle one. Is Thomas a woodworking hobbyist? Maybe he could build sets and staging and risers and camera platforms. Is he an electrician by trade? Maybe he could take on the responsibility of repair and maintenance of your sanctuary's lighting system. Or maybe he would do well in the video playback position, where he's popping DVDs in and out of the machine. Is there something you would like to do but are not sure where to start? Maybe Thomas is God's provision for that need.

Wrong Attitude

Stan is a know-it-all, constantly correcting others on the media ministry team. He destroys morale and no one wants to work with him. Cheryl is a party queen and babbles incessantly about her Saturday nights on Sunday morning, making other volunteers uncomfortable. George is a whiner, complaining about everything and everyone. Teresa doesn't seem to care if she does anything right. She ignores instructions and takes the easiest way out: "Hey, it's good enough for church work!"

These are the toughest cases, the ones that are most likely to result in that pink slip. Things to try:

- First, bathe the situation in prayer!
- Try to release your frustration and anger and view the person as a child of God.
- Get to know him or her a little better. Remember that as humans, our pain comes out in a variety of ways. A volunteer with bad attitude may actually

be a person in pain. Note: if you sense that a person is dealing with severe issues, such as alcoholism, drugs, an abusive relationship, or depression, talk to your pastor and get help for this person immediately. You may be the only one in that volunteer's life who notices what's going on.

- Talk to the person directly about the issue. Remain empathetic and ask for the person's own assessment of the situation.
- Share your point of view, without condemning. Assume that the person has no idea that his or her behavior has a negative effect.
- Make sure the volunteer understands the codes of behavior and attitude in your church and ministry. It may be that the person just doesn't understand or has never been told.
- Be very clear about what needs to happen, explain the bottom line, but focus on the ministry itself rather than the offending volunteer. You might say, "We want to maintain a positive environment for all the volunteers during weekend services" rather than "You have to stop correcting people and making them feel bad."
- Invite the volunteer to be part of the solution. Ask how you can help. Is a secret signal from you needed when he or she is getting close to the line? Is there another person in the ministry who might help you work with this person?

What if the person is belligerent, disagrees with everything you say, will not acknowledge his or her error, or is unwilling to discuss it with you at all? Use your best judgment. The person might need a little time to digest what's been said. If you think that's the case, **suggest** that the person think and pray about the conversation for a week and then set a time to meet again. If you don't think a week's time will help, or if the person is still unwilling at the second meeting, you need to release the volunteer. **Reiterate** the position, again focusing on the ministry, avoiding condemnation of the volunteer. **Acknowledge** that it's a difficult situation, and suggest that the volunteer might be happier and more productive serving elsewhere. **Clearly state** that, for the ministry's sake, you need to ask the volunteer to withdraw. If possible, have a specific idea or two of another area in the church where the volunteer might serve. Talk to the head of that ministry to determine if there's a need and if this person might be a good fit. Give the volunteer the contact information for that ministry area. **Suggest** that the person take a Spiritual Gifts course. Remind the person that, for many people, finding the right place to serve takes a little exploration. **Give** the volunteer some say in how the withdrawal happens. Consider how it might affect the team. **Agree** on a plan.

Know that these conversations are usually not as bad as our anticipation of them is. We've had to go through this several times with our media ministry, and in each case, the ministry and the volunteer both moved on in positive ways.

Chapter Four

A Professional Staff Matrix

For the purposes of this book we'll define staff as those people who draw a salary or regular hourly wages in exchange for their time spent serving in the media ministry. If your media ministry is just beginning, or if it's a small-medium operation, you probably don't have staff. Most or all of the work might be done by volunteers. At Resurrection, we produced video projects for several years before any staff was hired. We hired local news videographers to shoot the pieces and paid a local editorial facility to do the edits. Most of the people working in the media ministry during its first four years were volunteers. These dedicated servants did administrative, creative, and technical jobs.

At some point, you're likely to face decisions about paid staff like Resurrection did. A key decision you're likely to face is whether to change a volunteer job into a paid one. In fact, if you're heading up the media ministry, you might be serving in a volunteer capacity yourself, spending more and more hours at "work," wondering if it's not time for your volunteer job to be classified as a "real" one. This chapter offers some suggestions for making critical staff decisions.

A Matrix to Help

There are three basic questions to consider in a matrix to help decide whether it's time for a volunteer job to become a paid staff position. These questions include the number of hours required for the job each week, the on-site time required, and the need for accountability.

1. Number of hours required

- **Try** to identify the time that's really required, stripping away extras or add-ons. Let's say, for example, that you're considering making the graphics formatter a paid staff position. Let's assume you have a volunteer responsible for formatting the lyrics in the graphics sequence each week, but this person also coordinates the audio team schedule. As you think about the situation, separate the graphics tasks from the audio tasks. You might find that the groups of tasks can be divvied up differently. Maybe you need to hand off the audio team coordination to another volunteer. That might enable you to continue getting the jobs done with volunteers for a while longer. Sometimes all you need is to reorganize!

- **Sometimes** you just can't find a way to reorganize in order to get a job done. So, if a job takes more than ten to twelve hours per week, you should consider making it a paid position.

2. On-site time required

- **Evaluate** what sort of on-site time is required to do the job. Some tasks require someone to be at the church, either to do the work or to attend meetings. Many volunteer jobs can be done from home. Could

some tasks be done via e-mail? If so, maybe your volunteers could begin working that way, instead of coming to the church office. If volunteers don't have the necessary software or hardware at home, consider purchasing laptop computers for them to check out, enabling them to work at home. This will almost certainly cost less than a staff position.

- **Look** at some jobs that really do require on-site work hours: meetings where critical information is shared, a graphics system that "lives" in the church's technical booth, microphones and cables that must be repaired in the sanctuary. There's no way to export these tasks to a volunteer's home office or kitchen table. So, if a task requires a significant amount of time to be spent at the church, consider making it a paid position.
- **Note**: you will have to define "significant" for your ministry. Typically, a task requiring more than five hours per week could be considered significant. But this will vary from ministry to ministry and from volunteer to volunteer. You may have volunteers who are students or retirees or stay-at-home moms or dads of school-age children; these folks may want to serve ten or more hours per week as volunteers.
- **Explanations** can sometimes take longer than simply *doing.* "It's easier if I just do it myself." We've all said this from time to time, haven't we? And sometimes it's true. Occasionally, managing volunteers eats up too much of a staffer's time. **Loop** volunteers in! If you're finding that you spend inordinate amounts of time and energy explaining what's going on to volunteers, consider inviting them to be part of the process. Include them in meetings where decisions are made. Add them to e-mail distribution lists so that they receive information earlier. Hand off entire chunks of work to trusted

volunteers when possible; link them up with church staff as necessary to empower them to accomplish the tasks at hand. Make volunteers part of the process and not just part of the implementation. You'll spend less time explaining things to them, and they will be more fully vested in their ministry tasks. Sometimes you simply can't include volunteers in the day-to-day operation of ministry enough to keep them fully informed and equipped. So, if you determine that it's too great a drain on church staff time and energy to continue preparing a volunteer, consider creating a staff position.

3. Need for accountability

How much wiggle room is there for mistakes or no-shows or half-done work? When you're thinking about whether to switch a job from volunteer to staff, consider this: if there's enough leeway for mistakes to get fixed, for someone else to fill in, or for the task to be left undone, the job probably doesn't have a high need for accountability. But some jobs are so critical that they must be done at a certain time, in a certain way. Leaders and volunteers should hold one another accountable. But the dynamic is different between a staff person and supervisor; the lines of expectation and responsibility are sharper and usually stronger. There's no easy tip here; you will be the best judge of the need for accountability in the ministry's work. If a job is critical, it's critical and there's not much you can do to modify that short of lowering the bar. One thing to think about, however, is that jobs and expectations do change. A task that was not terribly critical a year ago might be essential, requiring a high degree of accountability today.

> So, if the job in question is critical, if bad things happen when it's not done on time in the right way, consider shifting it to a paid position.

If your answer to two or more of the criteria listed above leads to the conclusion of a paid person for the task, consider one more factor: do you choose a staff position or an outside contractor?

Staff Position or Contractor?

Maybe you should indeed consider creating a staff position. The next question is, "What kind?" At Resurrection, paid contractors have been economical and highly effective. With a contractor, you pay either an hourly rate or a predetermined fee.

Advantages:

Typically, the church doesn't provide permanent office space or benefits for contractors and contractors can be employed and released with fewer restrictions and less paperwork. In addition, church staff members are not generally obliged to closely manage contractors. For example, there are no yearly performance reviews, so contractors are less of a drain administratively and managerially. Often, highly skilled freelancers can be hired to do contract work, enabling the gain of higher-quality work than the church would be able to afford otherwise.

Disadvantages:

The hourly rates to be paid for contractors are generally higher than the hourly rate for regular church staff. Contractors are less likely to feel vested in the ministry and may contribute less to the spirit of the staff. There may be a lack of continuity in the ministry's work, especially if multiple contractors are used. Contractors may not be available when you want them to be, and they're under no obligation to make themselves available. Contractors may be more difficult to budget for; you must carefully estimate how they will be used and what they will likely cost. And at some point, because of the higher hourly rates, you may begin to spend more on contractors than you might on a full-time staff position.

If the media ministry is responsible for extra tasks such as special media projects or once-a-year events, consider hiring contractors to do some of the work. If the extras are more than your volunteers and regular staff can absorb, contractors might be the answer. Hire videographers, video editors, writers, graphic artists, audio engineers, lighting technicians, and producers to take on chunks of work, protecting your regular staff from dangerous overload. Staff and volunteers should be able to handle the regularly occurring workload. Consider contractors if you have special projects or tasks that are more than your volunteers and staff can manage.

Simple Staffing Strategies

Following are some ideas to try, concepts to keep in mind, and tips to remember as you build a media ministry.

- **Volunteers** can do amazing work. Many Resurrection media ministry staffers actually began as volunteers. Don't buy into the myth that only a "professional staff" can do media ministry.
- **Target** volunteers who are positive, bright, flexible, and willing to learn. Pour your knowledge and vision into these people and watch them serve the Lord in amazing ways. These should be the first people turned to for paid staff.
- **Choose** the unskilled person with a pleasant disposition if you have to make a choice between that person and the skilled person with a difficult personality. With a few exceptions, you can teach the skills.
- **Build** a team. When on the brink of change—a person leaves the team, or your ministry is given a

new set of responsibilities, or you're hiring a new staff person—is the time to take the opportunity to evaluate the team and shift it around to create new strength. Break it all apart in your mind and explore new ways of putting it back together to capitalize on the strengths of volunteers and staff, while filling in the gaps where weakest. Create a team with a good mix of work styles, personalities, and abilities. This kind of team will make ministry even more fun and will serve God more effectively in the long run.

- **Teach** people to champion others. I once hired a new staff person whose skills were not up to par in one area. (I hired this person because of other valuable attributes brought to the team!) Another staff member came into my office a few weeks later and suggested that I dismiss this new employee. Instead, I encouraged the long-time staffer to teach and mentor and coach the "new kid." It turned out to be a great strategy.
- **Use** a companion strategy to the one just above: sometimes it's smarter to hire teachable people with fewer skills but great potential than it is to hire an experienced pro who knows every trick in the book. The teachable person probably comes with a lower salary requirement, but more importantly, the teachable person can be *taught!* You have the opportunity to bring that staffer along in the way you need him or her to grow for the ministry and the church.
- **Look** on the flip side, however. Sometimes you simply need to hire the best skills available. This is typically true for technical jobs. A couple of examples are audio engineer or technical director positions. So, look for the delightful *and* highly skilled people in media ministries—they're out there!

- **Create a team** of friends. Share life with one another, enjoy fellowship, have fun together. Make sure there's someone on the team who is an instigator of fun.

- **Organize** retreats for your team. I recommend having one work/spiritual retreat and one day-of-fun retreat each year. The work/spiritual retreat might be an overnight at a local church campground. This is a great opportunity to do long-range planning, problem-solving, dreaming, and vision casting with the team. The day of fun might be a trip to a local amusement park, a lake, or other fun environment. Make this a true day away for fellowship—no work allowed.
- **Claim** the responsibility to shepherd and care for the novice believers. Encourage them to ask questions. Set clear and attainable expectations for their spiritual life and discipleship as well as for their work—and make sure they are supported in that journey. One of the sweetest days for me was when a person on our team came to me with the news that he had finally joined a small group in the church. The change in this person's life from the time he joined our team is awesome and as rewarding as anything else we've done.

- **Lead** by example. You already know this, but it's worth repeating: we cannot ask others to follow where we are not willing to lead. If things seem to be falling apart in the media ministry, if people are not getting along, if morale is low, if things are just not right, look first in the mirror. Is all well with your soul? Are you earnestly striving to live the life Christ calls us to live? Are you sharing your striving with the team? Leadership is a tricky thing. We must own it and live into it daily, even on the days when we feel rather Moses-ish—stuttering, unworthy, unconfident, unprepared, and full of doubt.

Working With Other Church Staff

I would like to offer a handful of strategies for working with other church staff.

1. Climb out of the silos. Silos are our tendency to build little walls around our ministries. We get protective and territorial and at the same time we tend to insulate ourselves from new or daunting demands. Sometimes we fail to look at our colleagues standing nearby. We need to look up, climb out, and break down the silo walls between ministries. We can't work well with one another if we don't know one another. In ministry, where we're sharing scarce resources and where we feel passionate about our mission, we need to be partners and friends. It's easier to make decisions together when we understand each other's needs. It's easier to prioritize for the church when we're unified in spirit and in love. It's easier to give and receive grace in an atmosphere of trust and friendship. It's easier to generate great ideas when the environment is open and honest and where sharing is valued. It's easier to carry our burdens when our colleagues come alongside us to share them, especially in prayer. Conversely, everything in church ministry is more difficult when we separate ourselves into self-contained units—the silos. Sometimes, nearly adversarial relationships start to fester. And these can poison our ability to serve.

2. Invite everyone to the table. Media ministries are often called on to produce and support events in the church. Too often, they're *not* called to the table during the planning stages for those events. That's the unfortunate cause of many problems when it comes time for implementation. Expectations and budgets are unrealistic. Key technical issues are overlooked. And good ideas are never heard. So, talk to whoever is responsible for event planning in your church and help that person understand that the media team should be part of the planning process for any event it will be asked to support.

3. Make customer service a priority. In nearly every church with a media ministry, that ministry serves other ministries. In the very earliest days at Resurrection, the media ministry only produced media for worship. At that time, our church didn't do large, technology-driven events. High tech for us was showing a homemade video from the VHS deck on the TV in the corner of the fellowship room. But as we grew, the media team began taking on more and more technological support. Today, the team supports literally every other ministry in the church, producing media projects for programming and producing events nearly every night of the week. It may seem odd to characterize your work as customer service, but that's an apt description. Do some thinking and praying and talking with others about what it means for your ministry to be successfully serving its "customers." Talk about it in those terms with the media team. And put into practice the actions that will help the media ministry serve well.

CHAPTER FIVE

Decisions, Decisions! Or, Choices You'll Make About Time and Money

My husband works as an advertising creative director. He writes and comes up with ideas for commercials. A long time ago, he told me about something his friend—also an ad guy—had shared with him. It's The Good/Fast/Cheap Triangle, and it's one of the handiest tools I know of in planning media ministry.

In media production, projects can be two of the following, and only two: *Good*, meaning the project is "on purpose" and meets the other principles in this book and it is of excellent quality. *Fast*, meaning the project takes less than the average amount of time to produce—new graphics design in a couple of days, a video shot and edited and fully produced in a five-day week, etc. *Cheap*, meaning the project incurs no exceptional costs above and beyond the normal costs of doing ministry—no freelancers need to be hired to do the work (unless this is your normal practice), no fees have to be paid in order to obtain media (unless this is your normal practice). Costs also include the human variety: the toll exacted from staff and volunteers. This type of cost is real and is even more important than monetary costs, but it's often overlooked in ministry planning.

Imagine that these three things each form one side of a triangle. The Good/Fast/Cheap Triangle. We apply the Triangle when considering any media production project, choosing which TWO sides we'll use. Understand, and help others to understand, that you can never do a project that's Good *and* Fast *and* Cheap. When planning your project, which one can you give up? Is it okay to spend the extra money to hire a freelancer to shoot the stewardship campaign video in order to get the quality you want on schedule? In this scenario, you're giving up **Cheap** to get **Good** and **Fast.** Or is it okay for the project's production values to be a bit less than usual in order to turn it around in short order with no additional expense? In this scenario, you're giving up **Good** to get **Cheap** and **Fast**. Or is it okay to press your volunteers into service for three weeknights in a row in order to produce a great special event in seventy-two hours? In this scenario, you're giving up the human type of **Cheap** in order to get **Good** and **Fast**. You get the idea. The Good/Fast/Cheap Triangle is a helpful tool for planning.

Some Parameters

At your fingertips is an incredibly influential tool; program directors, ministry leaders, pastors, and laity will all see ways that tool could empower their ministries. And you probably will too. If you're just starting media ministry in your church, you'll soon learn what those who've been at it a while know well: you can't do it all. So, you must define what you *will* do. If you are just starting out, you're most fortunate. You can define the parameters of the media ministry from the get-go. If you're already swimming along (feels like drowning, maybe, on some days) you should figure out a way to take this important action.

- **Define** the ministry's priorities. Review the purpose of your church and ministry. Make a list of the types of projects that are most directly linked to that purpose. Make a list of the types of projects that seem most removed from your church and ministry purpose. These may include projects that you're already working on.
- **Consider** the church's objectives or goals for the year ahead. These should be written out and agreed upon by the church council or other administrative body. Don't substitute your own ideas of what *should* be important. Are there specific strategies that are to be carried out? A capital campaign or other fundraising effort? The launch of a new program? A church-wide new initiative or major shift in focus? Media projects supporting these objectives should probably go on your "Do" list. Projects that don't fit neatly under these categories should go on the "Do Not Do" list.

This is not to say that you should never take on the nonpriority tasks. There are at least two good strategies for getting these jobs done without sacrificing your most critical tasks.

1. You may be able to assign these jobs to volunteers who are just learning the ropes. Imagine you're asked to videotape a meeting or presentation

so that those who couldn't attend can see it later. A task of this type is rarely a priority. But just because you can't make the job a priority for yourself doesn't mean it can't get done. Spend a bit of time with a new or young volunteer and assign this person the videotaping task. This is a great way to provide on-the-job training and maximizes the ministry's capacity. Make sure in cases like this to give support to the volunteer, making sure that the volunteer has everything needed to succeed with the project.

2. Another strategy to try is training volunteers from other ministries. If the Women's Ministry needs weekly support for a Bible Study program, but you're not able to justify it as a priority, work with that ministry to identify a handful of people who will be willing to learn to run it themselves. They will feel grateful to learn the skills and to serve their ministry in a unique way. Often, after they've learned to run a sound board or camera or graphics, these volunteers actually cross over to become volunteers for the media ministry as well as for their original ministry area. Everybody wins!

➪ **Don't be** the pioneer. This is a short and simple point, but an important one: don't be a guinea pig. When you're deciding what sort of equipment to buy, you will see lots of enticing gear—the newest, most advanced, most mold-breaking technology. Vendors, websites, and salespeople will work hard to convince you that you will be "behind" somehow if you don't buy the newest technology. But newest doesn't always equal best. Let others take the financial risks involved in trying out the newest gear. Instead, concentrate on what your ministry really needs to get the job done and to enable some growth. Remember that technology changes all the time; it's not as if you're completely missing the boat or stymieing the ministry' capacity for growth by opting for more tried and true solutions. Plan on investing in some new technology around every three years. Buy "last year's model" or equipment that has been well tested in the real world for at least a couple of years. You can be fairly sure that most of the major bugs have been worked out (on someone else's dime) and that the technology will serve your ministry well until the next wave of replacements occurs.

A Guide to Buying Gear

This section is intended to provide you with an overall framework for when you're considering equipment purchases. These decisions can be fraught with anxiety. We're spending money that's in short supply, and we want to be good stewards. At the same time, we have visions for our ministries, and we see how great technology can make those visions reality. Each church and media ministry has different needs and different budgets, so it's impossible to write out a "Buy This" list here. There is no easy answer, and we must each do the time-intensive work of establishing a vendor relationship, defining the need, researching options, testing, choosing and finally purchasing.

1. Establishing a vendor relationship

For most of us, the array of media ministry-related equipment is overwhelming. Even if you are very knowledgeable about one type of equipment—edit systems, for instance—you're probably lacking knowledge in other areas. You could spend a lot of time sorting through manufacturer's materials and other resources, learning the ins and outs of every piece of equipment you will need to use in media ministry. But there are capable people who can do that homework for you and who can partner with you as you make these important decisions. Unless you really have breadth and depth of knowledge—and especially if you're purchasing more than one or two pieces of equipment—you should establish a good relationship with a vendor in your area.

That word *partner* is key. Before you decide what camera and edit system to buy, you should first find a vendor you can trust. Call colleagues and professionals in media around your area. These might be media teachers at the local high school or college, or the administrators who are responsible for the media systems in the schools. Also contact local and regional television and cable stations. If there are any large advertising or public relations companies nearby, call them. Call large corporate offices and ask to speak to the head of their media department. All of these organizations will have worked with audio-video equipment vendors, and they will usually be happy to share their experiences.

Put together a list of the audio-video suppliers and reps who have gotten good marks and then start meeting with them.

Ask a lot of questions about how they work, what services they provide, and how they price their equipment and services.

- Which manufacturers do they work with?
- What can they bring to the table as far as design? If you're building a new system from scratch, or doing a major update to an existing system, you will benefit from a vendor who can do the design work for you.
- How much training will be provided for your team and what kind of training is offered?
- What sort of customer support is provided, for how long, and at what cost? Remember, you will likely need the most support on weekends when some vendors may charge additional fees. As you give the vendor these and other questions,

get a sense of what it would be like to work with this person and his or her company. A positive relationship with an excellent vendor will benefit your church for years to come as you build an effective media ministry.

Note: in churches with very large video installations, the design is often done by a firm specializing in that sort of work rather than by any one vendor. Then, the equipment may be purchased and installed through several vendors and installation companies.

2. Defining the need

Figure out what you need a piece of equipment to do. Be as specific as you can. Ask volunteers who are or will be responsible for operating the equipment to help you think this through. Make a list of the must-haves and separate list of the nice-to-haves. Remain objective and focused on the essential purpose of each item. Don't let cool bells and whistles dazzle you and don't let sticker shock immobilize you. (Like a good United Methodist, be methodical!) Start with the bottom-line task that needs to be done: graphics projected on screen during worship; camera shots of worship projected during worship, video clips projected during worship; and camera shots, graphics, and videos switched seamlessly back and forth during worship. For instance, when you're looking at graphics projection software, consider exactly what you need to be able to do. Will you need to be able to create a sequence in another program and transfer it to the graphics program? Will you need to import Photoshop files? Do you need to run video clips from this program, or do you have other playback equipment for that? When you're running the system during worship, what exactly will the operators need to see—a sequence list, thumbnail images

of each page, the current page and the one next in line, or a combination of these? Will you need to be able to make changes to the sequence while it's running? Will you need to be able to import pages from other sequences? These are only a few of the questions you might ask. The key is to ask them to define specifically what your church really needs.

3. Research

- **Use** the Internet to search out information about the equipment you seek. You will find product reviews, owner's manuals (a good way to see what it might really be like to use the gear), magazine articles, blog entries, warranty information, repair histories, and information on vendors selling the equipment. Print off anything that seems pertinent and create files for each type of equipment.
- **Visit** trade shows and expositions. These can be a good way to meet several vendors or manufacturer reps at one time. Gather lots of business cards and make notes on the back of each about your impressions of the company and its people. Often, you can get your hands on equipment for a convention-floor test run. This can serve as a sort of prescreening and saves time later by helping you avoid unnecessary demos back home. Keep in mind, conventions are a part of the research phase; don't buy gear there when you're likely to be swayed by snazzy displays and heavy sales pitches and "convention-only deals." Only gather information for later use.
- **Talk to** colleagues about what they use. Ask for equipment lists. Ask how the equipment has worked for them. What are the best and worst points? Would they buy this again? Were there

any surprises or unexpected problems? Did the manufacturer supply adequate training? What has the repair and maintenance history been like? Is it working the way colleagues thought it would, meeting the ministry's needs?

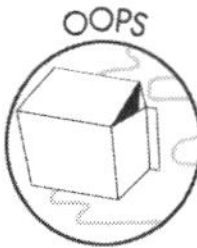

When we were working on the first camera purchases for Resurrection's media ministry, back in 1998, I was looking at two different camera options. I was certain that one option was the best and was ready to sign on the dotted line for it. Our vendor, however, strongly urged me to demo both cameras, side-by-side. He knew I needed to see firsthand the attributes of each camera and to see them in comparison. He was right, and I ended up choosing *against* the camera I thought we would buy. The other one worked just as well, had a couple of added features, and was *cheaper* than the one I'd originally favored. In the end, that was a great decision, and one I would have missed if I hadn't tested the cameras. At the writing of this book, those original cameras are still in use, having lasted twice as long as I expected. And yes, you read it right: the vendor *did* push me toward the less expensive option.

4. Testing and demos

Your next step is to give a list of good options a try. Ask your vendor to arrange a demo of the equipment you're considering. A side-by-side test, if possible, can be incredibly valuable. When you're testing gear, arrange for the folks who will be using it to test it with you. The graphics operator will pick up on things you miss, and the sound technician will understand the audio board's functionality in ways you might not. Your decision should be fairly straightforward. What works best and will supply the need for a cost that's within your budget?

5. Choosing: garbage in, garbage out

If you choose equipment and materials based solely on price tag, it will show up in the media you produce for your church. So, once you've defined the essential need, strive to get the best equipment you can afford. Don't settle for what's easiest or cheapest unless it *also* best meets the defined need for your ministry.

➪ **Equipment** lists. Since prices, model numbers, and specifications of equipment change from year-to-year, we will help you by keeping a fairly frequent update of equipment and costs on our Resurrection Web site at www.cor.org.

6. Purchasing

Purchasing the equipment is the easy part. Remember that for some pieces you may have to wait. Your vendor can help you know what to plan on; be sure to ask when delivery can be expected so that you can plan accordingly.

CHAPTER SIX

Media Ministry Is About People

It was an important Sunday. The stewardship campaign was in full swing, and Reverend Hamilton had prepared a great message; it was fast-moving with several production elements. It included object lessons requiring close-up shots of an old book, a handsaw, and a score sheet from a recent game of Hearts. Everyone in the room needed to be able to see and understand the lessons. The pastor would preach from several scripture passages, so graphics were critical. We were trying something new with lighting for the praise and worship set, so we needed a couple of extra people on the light board.

In the basement media control room, Kevin, the graphics operator, had discovered a problem with the week's sequences. They had not been saved correctly, or maybe the system had malfunctioned. But all the backgrounds were wrong, rendering some of the lyrics and other text illegible. He was frantically correcting them, slide by slide. He doubted he would get them all fixed in time, but was making a valiant effort.

It was about thirty minutes before the service would start when the switcher suddenly, inexplicably stopped working.

Brett, the volunteer technical director that day, methodically pushed every button, hoping that a simple stuck button was causing the problem. When that didn't work, he shut down the machine, issuing a quiet but intense statement of warning to no one in particular: "The switcher has failed. I'm rebooting and will let you know what happens." For a moment, most of the eight people busily working in the room stopped checking graphics, adjusting camera color, marking scripts, and cueing tapes in order to absorb this news.

A minute or so later Tisha, the camera team leader, popped her head in the door and made the morning's second work-stopping announcement: "We have only one camera operator! Jim just called to say he's sick, Pete is out of town and I don't know where his sub is and I have no idea where Betsy is and can't get her on the phone." A dull, faint groan rolled around the room.

Five minutes later, the control room crew had finished their preservice checks and other preparatory tasks; they filtered out into the hallway for the crew call meeting. All but Brett, who was now on his cell phone talking to the vendor, trying to troubleshoot the switcher. The reboot had not worked. The director led his teammates through the day's rundowns, noting everything they would need to remember. After they shared joys and concerns around the circle, they prayed. Then they scattered quickly to their posts. The sanctuary was full, and worship would begin in eight minutes. Brett had gotten the switcher back on, but it was acting strange, not dissolving correctly and glitching. We had only one camera operator, and all the other cameras were in lock-down. We could use them, but only the shots they were locked in on. This would restrict our ability to shoot the service well and might even be distracting for the congregation. As the prelude ended and Reverend Hamilton stepped up to welcome the congregation . . .

I'm afraid I've fooled you a little since with this scenario. It's ficticious, but it is a combination of events and circumstances that really happened in our church at one time or another. The frenzy and anxiety may seem familiar to you. I hope that the resolution does, too, because this story has a good ending like our stories normally do. Kevin fixed all the graphics. They looked great, were easy to read, and helped the congregation worship. Brett's persistence was more powerful than the switcher; he kept it functioning through the service without missing a take. And about ten minutes into the program, we noticed that all three of the locked-down cameras were moving. Three volunteers who were here to worship noticed the vacant camera positions, and each took one.

Four Important Things

- **Media** ministry is more about people than it is about media. All the true-life characters in this story are volunteers. And among them only one had professional experience in media. The others had no experience until they began serving in our media ministry. **Media ministry can be operated primarily with volunteers.** Furthermore, most of the people in this story were either non- or nominally religious when they first came to the church and to our ministry. Sure, they learned how to shoot video and create graphics and troubleshoot complex equipment like video switchers. But most importantly to them and to the church—they grew into Christians who know God with their minds, love God with their hearts, and serve God with their hands.
- **Now** and then, visit the mountaintop**.** You will plan, work hard, set goals, and constantly strive to improve the media ministry's effectiveness for your church, I hope. You'll keep your nose to the grindstone for weeks at a time and will feel like you're constantly putting out fires. You'll be leading people

in change, which can be mentally and emotionally exhausting. Sometimes, you'll feel like you're running hard but getting nowhere, standing still. Endure a couple of mornings like the one described above, and you'll begin to feel worn out. You begin to feel frustrated and impatient. After a few weeks like this, it's easy to forget the successes you've had, the things that have gone well, and the people who are such a gift all around you. That graphics system might have been slightly quirky, but the graphics team—magicians, really—create beautiful images and text every week. The switcher may have gone on the fritz, but—for goodness sake—*we had a switcher!* And the camera operators might occasionally not show up, but most weeks—52 weeks a year, 4 services a week, 208 times each year, plus special events—there were 4 volunteers on camera with cheerful hearts and steady hands. *That's more than 832 camera operators!* Only a couple of years earlier, we had a very limited graphics system, with static blue backgrounds every week, a router only (no switcher), and one camera. We had a lot to be grateful for, if only we could stop to remember it. Sometimes we need to take in that mountaintop view, where we can "see" how far we've come, in order to keep marching forward on the trail in front of us.

- **Focus** on purpose. This has nothing to do with the relative clarity and crispness of video images, of course. It has everything to do with the ministry's reason for being—your purpose. Media ministry should not exist in your church for the wrong reason. If the ministry is not about kingdom work, if the people in it are not striving to accomplish something that is part of the church's larger vision, it will likely fail. And days like the one described above will hasten that failure. This work can be anxiety producing, with its constant deadlines and unpredictable technical problems. It takes time and energy. No one will hang around for too long if there's not a clearly defined, noble purpose for the work. The ministry's purpose must come directly from your church's purpose, and the work of the ministry should be defined by that purpose. Period.

➪ **Keep** God in your gizmo! Actually, God is already there, and *that* is the real point. Sometimes, the best thing you can do is to remember that, no matter what, God will show up for worship. If every piece of equipment fails, if the lights go out, if the sound system goes down, and if no volunteers show up to run camera, God will still be there. It's easy to get confused about the importance of our work. It *is* important. But its importance comes from the reason we're there, not from the cool gear or fun people or the video production adrenaline rush—Christians have worshiped God for centuries without any technology at all. The funny thing is that, in my experience, God typically bails us out even when we don't expect it. The missing camera operator situation has occurred often over the last decade, but we never went through an entire service without the necessary cameras. Volunteers stop by to say hi or to see if there is anything they can do—even on their "off" days. Whether you believe that God actually sent those volunteers to check in on those days or whether you believe that God has simply infused the ministry with a deep sense of commitment, I have seen over and over that God is in our midst, and that God provides what we need to serve him. So, remember the God you worship and may you know God's blessings in the media ministry you work in and in your life.